HUGS

POEMS

Psalm 91:4

HE covers me
with HIS feathers
and under HIS wing
I will trust.

by Virginia Dickson

HUGS

Virginia Dickson

GREAT PRAISE AND THANKS TO
JESUS CHRIST FOR GUIDING US

HELPING YOU BUILD YOUR DREAM WITH INK!

For every book sold 10% Goes to the United Church Charity Fund.

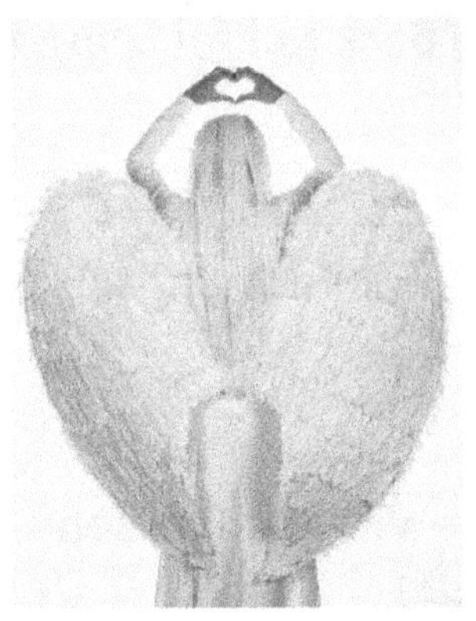

HUGS

†

These poems are like medicine to the broken hearted in life, bound by addictions, pain and every mental torment. Some of these poems are my Holy Spirit counseling sessions with the Lord, some are a testament to His goodness put into poetry. They shine the light of Christ into the dark side of self, exploding it and showing the way to be free. GOD is the very essence and SPIRIT of LOVE; Beloved is what He calls you; allow Him to love you back to life! Learn to trust again!

Love in Christ!

Virginia Dickson

50 HUGS

THE FIRST BOOK OF MOSES, CALLED

GENESIS.

CHAPTER 1

IN the * beginning † God created the
heaven and the earth.   * John 1. 1, 2.
    † Ps. 8. 3, & 33. 6, & 89. 11, 12, & 102. 25.
    ‡ Heb. 1. 10.   Is. 44. 24.   Jer. 10. 12, & 51. 15.
    136. 5, & 146. 6.   Acts 14. 15, & 17. 24.   Col. 1. 16, 17.   Heb.
    ‡ch. 12. 1.   11. 3.   Rev. 4. 11, & 10. 6.

2 And the earth was without form, and
void ; and darkness was upon the face
of the deep.   * And the Spirit of God
moved upon the face of the waters.
    * Ps. 33. 6.   Is. 40. 13, 14.

3 * And God said, † Let there be light:
and there was light.   * Ps. 33. 9.   † 2 Cor. 4. 6.

4 And God saw the light, that it was
good : and God divided * the light from
the darkness.
    * Heb. between the light and between the darkness.

5 And God called the light * Day, and
the darkness he called Night.   † And
the evening and the morning were the

INTRODUCTION

From the Publisher:

This book is a classic case of how in our darkest moments of despair, can emerge the glory and salvation of Jesus Christ. Through His guidance we can easily transform pain into blessings.

Just before meeting Virginia Dickson, my faith, belief, and communion with Christ had just rekindled. I had a vision of Jesus giving me a hug… It was the most loving presence I had felt. I even cried for a while! It was powerful! Almost right after this experience, I met Virginia. She told me she wanted to write a book about Jesus, called *"Hugs."* Needless to say, I knew I had to publish this book! How many signs, omens, or pointers do you need!?

This book has the power to change your life. It has the means and holy intention to bring the reader closer to an intimate loving relationship to Jesus Christ. When Virginia mentions her "intimate connection" with Jesus, she is talking about how the Spirit moves her, inspires her, and how she has taken responsibility for what Christ has given her. With a courageous heart aligned with the will of God; Virginia has written these pages so that others too can find Christ in their times of need. So others too, can return to the source of perfection.

This book intended to help those lost find a Shepard, those addicted, to find serenity, for those stressed to find peace, for those in doubt to find faith, for those troubled minds to again open-up and realize the divine guiding light shinning upon all of us. Just thinking about and talking with Jesus in an open way, allows us to open-up to the empowering ideas of salvation, love, faith, compassion, healing, and everything Christ has risen for!

Indeed, greatness calls to everyone, but not everyone listens. Virginia has devoted herself to that softest yet mightiest voice. She has taken responsibility and answered the call. I am grateful for these channels that God has inspired through Virginia; to open up miracles in the lives of those touched by this precious gift. Thank (y(O)u), God, for inspiring Virginia with all these great works.

God Bless & Enjoy!

LOVE IN CHRIST

1. **Christ Kissed**

Reborn of GOD, meek not wild,

I surely must be GOD's favourite child,

Jesus came and rescued me from the world,

Now my voice causes Hell to be unfurled,

Preparing me for that wedding feast,

He gives power to the weak and least,

A chosen generation for such a time as this,

When you accept Christ's intimate kiss,

Living a love song that goes on and on,

Intimacy that reaches deep inside my being,

Permitting me, Third Heaven seeing,

Oh, how I love Him so very much,

For the essence of Heaven is in His touch,

In His blood atonement, I am highly priced,

For I've received that intimate kiss from CHRIST,

2. **The Daisy Game**

Hold my hand, caress my cheek,

Verify love, for I am lonely and weak,

After many years of marriage,

Intimacy has a miscarriage,

Years go by playing the daisy game,

But day after day it stays the same,

No kisses or hugs, compassion traces,

Petrified, to enter the pain places.

When JESUS sings His love song,

My heart enjoys to sing along,

Until my heart is fully blessed,

Leaving behind rejections pest,

Learning, growing, loving GOD,

Jesus intimacy as I walk this sod,

3. **Heaven's Kiss**

When your husband no longer shows affection,

And you nurture the spirit of rejection,

Seeking GOD's answers from above,

Knowing He is the author of true love,

A covenant vow made in marriage,

Does not have to end in a miscarriage,

Back when GOD created the universe,

He created, checked and chose me first,

Now through Christ I've reversed the curse,

My Being is oiled each day by His Spirit,

Living out my purpose with Jesus merit,

Now I've chosen Him above all other,

He has opened Heaven for me to discover,

He sings a love song each night to me,

And His holy hugs set me free, to be,

What a LOVER I would have missed,

I'm redeemed, loved and Heavenly kissed,

4. **Scars**

I came to GOD with all my scars and bruises,

And found out that is exactly what He uses,

I showed Him mine, and He showed me His,

Mine simply vanished, what a wonderful quiz,

Coming to end of self, allows Him to begin,

Now He lives in me, and I live in Him,

What an exchange, living out of a Sacred Place,

Praying with Jesus for the whole human race,

Now I know that's what my wounds where for,

Resting in Him, growing and craving for more,

Now He fights my battles and settles the score,

Living out my life on His beautiful plain,

Divinely healthy, well and soundly sane,

5. **Repent**

As I knelt and poured out my heart to GOD,

To take possession of this miserable Sod,

To really know the power of His salvation,

To come in and make me a new creation,

That day Christ was born in my heart and soul,

He washed me clean and made me whole,

My eyes saw clearer at every glance,

The leaves on the trees seemed to dance,

And all the birds sang a new song,

I heard the voices of an angel throng,

At salvation don't stop as petrified,

Christ's purposes first, life is gratified,

His nature now invites me to impart,

To perform the vision planted in my heart,

I realized life was an abstract myth in religion,

A mistaken taught, intangible condition,

Divine realities from GOD, I am now filling,

For all glory to GOD, I am willing,

6. **Fornication**

Older women still need their husband's touch,

For she still loves him so very much,

But he gets off playing dangerous games,

In his mind reminiscing on younger dames,

The demons torment and guilt pursues,

But he has a need for his mind to muse,

Holiness, he tries to show, bible reading has to go,

Way too much guilt and condemnation,

Causing division in their marriage relation,

Prayer warriors fight the spiritual battle,

That cage he is in starts to rattle,

A miracle as the Holy Ghost pursues,

This fight in man's soul, GOD will not lose,

Free will is still his, it is time to choose,

"Demons must go," is the battle cry,

GOD knows, the choice is his to live or die,

7. **When Angels Cry**

When a fetus is cut from a mother's womb,

The flesh discarded in a garbage can tomb,

Angels take the little spirit soul back to GOD's arms,

Rescuing them, setting off Heavens alarms,

At such a mission Angels cry; asking why?

GOD's plans for Preachers, Leaders and such,

Now their cast away, as fears motives touch,

Precious woman, GOD also sees your broken heart,

Angels where assigned to you from your very start,

Repent and run into the Fathers open arms,

In billows of love, erasing all earthly harms,

Oh! Remember created, Beloved woman child,

Christ paid your sin debt, from choices made wild,

Forgive yourself, Jesus took all your guilt and wrath,

Precious One, change your own chosen path,

GOD does not condemn so His love will abound,

Into that human heart where He is found,

Receive Heavenly hugs, your child is living,

Angels are tending, playing, laughing and giving,

8. Jesus Step In

Follow Me one step at a time,

I'll make your life a beautiful rhyme,

Simply trust, don't ask why,

Step out, I'll teach you to fly,

Walk by faith, not by sight,

Spread your wings I'll give you flight,

Don't worry about cliffs ahead,

Your covered, trust Me instead,

My angels keep you in all your ways,

Guarding steps to end of your days,

I AM your strength and shield,

Your part is to simply yield,

Take time to renew your mind,

Opening sight, to ways your blind,

You were born to be My Lover,

Heart and purpose of GOD to discover,

To walk this earth to simply be,

A living replica of Me,

9. **Override**

I am computer minded, as I live my day,

Evaluating what people do and say,

But when others are in your face,

Lean on GOD'S amazing grace,

At these times pride is dangerous,

Humility is aware of who lives in us,

Humble yourself in GOD'S might,

His Holy Spirit gives matured insight,

Immediately down load a prayer or verse,

Putting that anger in reverse,

For GOD gives you the ability,

To cloth yourself with humility,

This act puts Satan on stall,

Waiting for GOD'S timing, in the long hall,

So when put to the test, override the flesh,

YOUR -MIND------- REFRESH!

Speaking out words of love, not hate,

Fulfilling GOD'S plan, your predestined fate,

10. **Frantic Calls**

Mary's frantic calls, Jesus, Jesus, creates a fuss,

But family and friends prove he is not among us,

One day out from Passover, turns into three days of panic pleas,

Jesus was found in the temple, teaching priests, if you please,

In my Father's house, did you not know where I would be?

Opening eyes and inspiring hearts, so they could see,

Are you found with no peace; is Jesus lost?

Jesus, Jesus, is your pain's cry from sin's cost,

Keep searching and seeking because of your lack,

And softly and quietly He will come back,

Bow in humble repentance and soon you will find,

Jesus is home again in your heart, calming your mind,

Intimate talks with Jesus and you won't want to stray,

He'll quietly walk beside you, showing the way,

11. **The Secret Place**

God meets you in a stilled, quiet, place within,

Where you surrender all worldly cares and sin,

Open your soul to Jesus the Precious One,

Receive the blood atonement of God's own Son,

The Father is delighted when you create a quiet place to meet,

There, devil's arrows you'll learn to defeat,

He knows the effort it took to quiet your soul,

Allowing the Spirit to make you whole,

A thirst for God's words increase, walking in the way,

He will open your heart to flow in God's DNA,

All fleshly lust there will be no more trace,

With your daily visit to the Secret Place,

12. **Voices**

Walking through the wilderness path,

Letting go of all wrongs and wrath,

Hearing birds calling one to another,

It's really God calling you lover,

He speaks through nature, and scripture,

Holy Spirit whispers, not a lecture,

He holds the skies in His big hand,

And in the other oceans grand,

God is all around you if only you'll listen,

From star lit sky, to dawn's early glisten,

So know God is beside you through life's walk,

His voice gently guides you, He'll quietly talk,

So don't run through life and never discover,

The voice of God, for He calls you Lover,

13. **Simple Sheep**

I am content to be a simple sheep,

God's word to keep,

Listening for His voice, and follow,

In green pastures wallow,

When attacked keeping silent,

So God can fight the battlement,

Speaking God's word to the bad thought,

Pulling thoughts , Satan has rot,

Walking on this freedom path,

No condemnation, guilt or wrath,

Taking the righteous path, for His name sake,

He restores my soul, confusion to take,

Fearing no evil as I go, for my cup is on overflow,

Knowing God is with me every step of life's way,

Goodness and mercy are here to stay,

Until forever in the house of the Lord, dwell,

That is the hope that keeps me will,

14. **Rhythm of Grace**

Living in the rhythm of grace, gives fear no place,

Come to Me, Jesus said, peace plays a lullaby instead,

Nothing can separate you from Me,

Regardless of feelings, give thanks and you will see,

I'll give you joy unspeakable, when all says it's unreachable,

Continual praise rises up from your heart,

In tune with Me from new days start,

Walking through life to the beat of a different drum,

Leaves no time for circumstances to make you glum,

I'll plant little pleasures along your path,

So forgiveness comes instead of wrath,

Frowns become smiles, you'll simply be,

Enjoying the rhythm of grace, lived through ME,

15. **Wonderful**

Jesus died to set me free,

What greater love can there be,

Truths freedom is sometimes hard to face,

Walking daily by His grace,

Completing each task that each day brings,

Causes joy to erupt and my heart sings,

Leaving behind rejections sting,

Thanking God for the pain places,

Drawing me into GOD'S embraces,

Talking in early morning conversation,

Starting my day with new revelation,

Christ is always the way, the truth, my salvation,

Now I can handle whatever life brings,

Christ is my strength, He gives me wings,

16. **Choose Life**

Father, draw me into the realm of your love,

Like a whirlpool flooding from above,

Fighting battles from GOD's resting place,

Eliminating time and space, and the world's rat race,

Where there are no backward glances,

Like a clock ticking forward, removing chances,

Giving hope substance into our world's time,

Fulfilling Your purpose, completing life's rhyme,

Heaven in me, right here on Earth,

Giving salvation a human place to birth,

I am loved, redeemed, in Jesus abound,

GOD saved me, my heart has been found,

17. **Skyler's Bubble**

Grandma, Grandma, Skyler calls,

Demons bouncing off the walls,

Evil voices hinder sleep,

Skyler sees into the deep,

Grandma calls Jesus into the room,

To rid the place of voices of doom,

Sleep now Skyler, Grandma says,

Jesus sprinkles holy water on devil's plays,

With a whimper and a pout,

Jesus cast the demons out,

Sweet sleep Skyler, HE surrounds him in a bubble,

Those demon will give you no more trouble,

I'll come back Jesus promised,

Struggles and pain day after day,

Ended in a hospital stay,

Jesus hugged and Holy Ghost Kissed,

On earth Skyler will be dearly missed,

In Heaven there is no sickness or disease,

Life is lived with greatest ease,

Now he is walking tall, playing on Jesus team,

Where streets are gold and angels stream,

It is not ours to question what GOD has done,

A reservation kept with GOD's own SON,

18. **Unclean**

The smell of death follows me,

No more cries inside to plea,

Twelve years of torment, my destiny,

Unclean, my identity,

All self effort gone, remain in chains,'

Yet hope for Messiah still remains,

In the silent nights lonely despair,

The touch of GOD knows I'm there,

Death or life is the same thing,

Messiah coming, gives faith a ring,

My last chance is passing me by,

Crawling, reaching in souls last try,

One leap of faith touched Jesus wing,

Causing a power surge to sing,

Jesus asks, where did my virtue go?

Come forth, for I must surely know,

At HIS feet I humbly explain,

To be risen, to live once again,

In one heart - beat, our hands meet,

Daughter, in wholeness go in peace,

The love of GOD to others release,

19. **The Antidote**

Do you have a silent scream held out of frustration?

When loved ones bring you tribulation,

Doing what's right, but it turns out wrong,

Holding back the victory song,

Being nice and always giving,

For Jesus inside is doing the living,

For a tear not cried can not be wiped,

GOD sees your heart, you've been skyped,

Ask and it will be given you,

Knock and the door will open too,

Why is Jesus the last resource?

When in reality, He is the source,

For the Holy Spirit goes where no man can go,

He releases that tear to flow,

Uplift in prayer and in love let them know,

Their choices and behavior has to go,

Jesus took it all on the cross, it has to flee,

GOD fights my battles, can you see,

Praise His name, He sets me free,

20. **Hope**

The love tones of God's voice,

Captures my soul, giving right choice,

Transforming you, with a new mind,

No condemnation of any kind,

Learning to live in holy living,

Growing in praying and giving,

Worry and fear are things of the past,

Devotions with Jesus, is power to last,

Allowing GOD to flow, happy and free,

I live in Him, and He lives in me,

Spirit walking, I found joy and peace,

Giving my flesh, a new step and increase,

GOD reigns over my thoughts and words,

No greater love song have I ever heard,

Learning to tell the Jesus story,

Christ in me, my hope of glory,

21. **4 AM**

Silent and calm at 4:00 in the morn,

Communing with Jesus, as He heals what is torn,

Quick to surrender into the arms of peace,

Forgiven to forgive, for my soul to release,

Offense and wrongs have no place to cry,

Stomp on the devil, don't even ask why,

For God gives me wings, so with eagles I'll fly,

No room for offenses to smolder and brood,

Allowing God's love call to change my mood,

God provides even birds with twigs for nests,

What greater provision, you are blessed,

Holy Spirit good morning, have your own way,

So I can sing praises all through my day,

22. **Spirit Walking**

Holy Spirit walking, is a freedom path,

Getting rid of all guilt and wrath,

Each morning take a cup of health and wellbeing,

Feeding on God's word, your truly seeing,

The Holy Spirit takes you deeper,

Giving real communion with your Keeper,

Putting an end to the Grim Reaper,

Diligently guard your heart,

Take thoughts captive from the start,

So calm your fears and worldly clatter,

For Jesus is the just of the matter,

Renewing your mind every step of the way,

And you will have a victorious day,

In continual praise, to thine own self be true,

By letting JESUS take care of you,

23. **Spirit Talking**

Speaking through the Spirit in conversation,

Right to GOD'S ears in communication,

As you get rid of the world's pollution's,

GOD speaks in a soft voice, giving solutions,

Spirit singing to the King of kings,

Angel's hear and Heavens harmony rings,

Release the fear; let your mind go free,

In your Spirit language, make your plea,

For supernatural things have not ceased to be,

Demons are confounded as He speaks to me,

Allowing the Holy Spirit to fill me up,

As peace, love and joy fill up my cup,

In your prayer language, take time to talk to GOD,

He'll give life's answers as you walk this sod,

Going about your day, letting GOD lead the way,

Intimacy will increase, and you will find,

Your powerful voice of the SPIRIT kind,

24. **Supernatural**

The calm assurance of your love,

Brings peace that echoes from above,

The Spirit speaks in whispers grand,

I have you safely in My hand,

Reassured and calm my heart beats strong,

As Angels minister the Spirits song,

Always kiss Me good morning first,

With My powerful word, I'll quench your thirst,

Water flow from deep within, taking the ways of f sin,

That Spirit river flows from a Heavenly portal,

Supernatural powers into this mere mortal,

25. **Joy's Response**

Rejection can become a stronghold,

Fight back with word spoken bold,

Tongues in intercession to torn emotion,

Giving Spiritual balm as healing lotion,

Joy level does not rely on others,

Putting Christ second the Spirit smothers,

Be responsible for your own joy,

The riches of your salvation is no ploy,

Cultivate and wear your righteous robe,

Looking unto GOD, Who holds this globe,

Knowing a perfect, constant Lover,

True joy of life is yours to discover,

26. **The Lion of Judea**

I am a child of GOD,

Walking through life on this sod,

Dark powers continually stalk,

Faith words, release the Lion,

As Demons flee and bock,

Bold prayers disperse Satan's evil hook,

They don't stay for a second look,

Fear and trembling is for them to be,

For the Lion of Judea lives in me,

Boldness in Christ is a learned response,

It is a weapon, not a flaunts,

Battling in Christ is our right,

So release the Lion to fight the fight,

With a roar, and a prayer lift up your rod,

Stand back and watch the power of GOD,

27. **Purpose**

As a new little spirit sits on GOD's lap,

Formed to fulfill purpose on the worlds map,

As the Father decides what will you be,

A Mother, Teacher, who makes the world see,

But because He created us to have our own will,

Patiently waiting, for His Spirit to fill,

Born into a world of sin, guilt and regret,

Stopping Satan's pull is the best choice yet,

Living in this realm was critical and stressing,

Life is a circle, exchanging the curse for blessing,

Choosing His purpose and plan just for me,

A blood bought decision, sitting back on GOD's knee,

28. **Love The NOW**

Has your heart been wrung out,

The circumstances make you pout,

Rejected by the ones you boast,

Still faithful is Christ your host,

Trusting your heart to the best,

As Jesus helps you pass the test,

Forgiveness reigns, taking the pain,

His calm assurance makes you sane,

In the now, that in between places

Birth to death, is the human race,

Bur living life to a Heavenly sound,

Hearing Loves call I abound,

Jesus experienced emotions of man,

So if he overcame, He says I can.

The father so loves all of mankind,

Breaking chains of addictions that bind,

Free and well and knowing inside,

Intimacy with Christ is how to abide.

29. Be Aware

Past pain kills your vision,

Satan haunts to create division,

Only GOD can fix past stuff,

It's hanging on that makes life ruff,

Enemy knows your weak places,

Putting you through your paces,

Some things you need to run from,

Danger lurks, and demons come,

Do not be found flirting with sin,

It will come out and give you a bite,

Then fear is given a home to fright,

Stop giving your heart to anyone,

Safe in the hand of GOD'S own Son,

Guard your heart and keep your vision,

For your heart CHRIST died, and is risen,

So ask Him in and you will find,

A whole new life of a different kind,

30. **Keeping Watch**

Protect the Sacred Place within,

Purify your heart from fear and sin,

Be careful little ears what you hear,

Be careful little eyes where you peer,

Thoughts unguarded, might dabble and play,

Leading you down a dark pathway,

Pits are waiting for you to fall in,

So don't give the devil a place to win,

Renew your mind in truth of GOD's word,

Rightly dividing the word you have heard,

Daily walking with Jesus your Lover,

Awesome, amazing things, you will discover,

You're not alone and never is it boring,

For on eagles wings you'll be soaring,

If you'll take time in His Secret Place,

Giving love to the whole human race,

And discover, to your own self be true,

By keeping watch, over who lives in you,

31. **The Journey**

Thank-you Lord, You designed time to protect me,

The rugged path has been steep, but now my journey I flee,

I look not behind, but ahead, focusing on Jesus instead,

Resting in You a while, until my heart can smile,

Being equipped to face whatever lies before,

One day at a time to live what Your plan has in store,

No rush, unlimited time, to meet You in this moment sublime,

Drinking deeply of Your presence, simulating Your essence,

The highest trust, not a request, but a must,

Knowing Jesus is with me where ever I go,

Secure when my journey takes me low,

32. **Bible**

I do not read a first-grade reader,

But a spirit, soul, life giving feeder,

The bible is GOD's love letters to you,

Resting, in a sovereignty that's true,

For it is about what I allow my eyes to see,

And what GOD says I am to be, we agree,

Fear comes, listening to what men say,

Faith comes, hearing GOD, showing the way,

Own your own sight and give fear flight,

GOD's words are life to those that find them,

Health to all their flesh, from stern to stem,

You may think oh stupid, or ugly me,

But never ever let your mouth agree,

Beautiful within, GOD's image created,

For Heaven's book, my name is slated,

Trying to fulfill the purpose of GOD,

Sometimes by myself, as I till this sod,

Know who you are above all else,

For the one you listen to most, is self,

33. **The Love War**

Oh, that I might walk in realms of love,

Be captured by God's Holy Dove,

When doing right, turns out wrong,

May I be found singing a praise song,

Where do you go when loved ones depart?

And you are left with a broken heart,

Tears captured in tissues by the case,

Resting in God makes me a new race,

Years pass by in a high, low state,

Knowing, I am master of my own fate,

Sorrows pass and grieving will cease,

Then you get a glimpse of peace,

Your soul jumps in, taking body, spirit, mind,

To walk life out, a higher kind,

Surrendering the flesh and emotions past,

Only Jesus love, brings healings that last,

Looking back only on things that make a smile,

Earth bound, but walking the golden mile,

34. **Open Heaven**

Holy, Holy, Holy, with the Angels I sing,

Rejoicing in knowing my King,

Taking time out to stop and pray,

Renewing my mind each new day,

Feeding from the fountain of God,

Under an open Heaven, walking this sod,

God keeping me from harm and strife,

Learning to dance, as I live this life,

Circumstances have no bearing,

Fighting the battles; in supernatural flaring,

Sometimes that old fresh brakes my stay,

Quickly bow in communion, and return in way,

Being happy is a choice only I can make,

Choosing what's best for Jesus sake,

For I live in Him and He lives in me,

Rejoicing, in all GOD's authority,

35. **Returning**

Precious Jesus who takes my pain and fears,

With Holy Ghost hugs collects my tears,

Loving has torn my poor heart in two,

MY pleading prayers trying to find You,

Come Holy Spirit until I sing Your song,

Hold me close, repenting all my wrong,

Diamonds are made under pressure,

Coming forth as diamond not lesser,

Trusting my heart to the Love that's true,

God always sees into the true you,

Loving the One who loves me most,

Father, Son, and Holy Ghost,

For Jesus shed His blood, for such as I,

Why, such love always makes me cry,

36. **Judas Kiss**

How to handle a kiss from Judas,

A trusted friend, sent to delude us,

Divulging pain places to others ear,

Are things only GOD's ear should hear,

Trust in GOD not in man,

Forgiveness comes, only if Holy Spirit can,

Just step back and bow to pray,

GOD will always show you the way,

As my soul thirsts for the Lord,

Lifting my spirit in one accord,

Grace dances around me, until I can see,

Religious people are a sad lot,

To be favoured they scheme and plot,

GOD sees the heart of the matter,

Collecting tears that gossip scatter,

Satan wants to destroy, lie and kill,

A Judas kiss, means your in-GOD's will,

37. **Heart**

The heart of man is exceedingly wicked,

It is enough to make your body sicked,

So Jesus came to change that way,

Gives transfusions with GOD's DNA,

Through life's journey, trials and pain,

Lift up worship! It will keep you sane,

He'll hold your hand and see you through,

For the heart of GOD is seeking you,

Bow to Christ, as He died on that tree,

A new creation, Born again to truly see,

Spirit hearing with your heart, really listen,

Hear GOD's word until you glisten,

For the heart of the matter is really this,

To intimate Ones, He gives His Holy kiss,

38. **Released**

A plagued soul lives in silence,

Seems your always paying penance,

Intimidated, tormented pain places,

Trying so hard to keep up with life's paces,

Chained, shackled, you can't even spit,

Until release comes and you simply quit,

Deciding to walk by faith and not by sight,

Putting life in tune and demons to flight,

A constant love song, Jesus reminisces,

Deleting past with GOD hugs and kisses,

For GOD designed this child for peace,

Simply give it all up to God and release,

I was so vulnerable to the devil's deceit,

Now I am shielded, empowered, complete,

39. **Soon**   John 8:29

The Father God hugs His Son in a Holy union,

And the two become one in communion,

In a Holy hue, whispering Revelation word,

That Jesus Christ alone has heard,

As Jesus turns and looks toward Earth,

His final love call, given birth,

The Holy Spirit reveals a warning to His church,

Return wanderer, don't be in the lurch,

Be ready, prepared, clean hands, clean heart,

Repent, be humbled, is a good place to start,

Jesus welcomes you into His love embrace,

Empowered, forgiven, releasing your enemy's case,

Living life in a whole new realm,

Now, Jesus Christ is at the helm,

Hosting His presence as we walk this land,

Until we are called up, by the Father's right hand,

At a trumpet sound, the dead in Christ shall rise first,

Then those who remain, through the clouds will burst,

We shall meet our Savior in the air,

Forever with Jesus, for war to prepare,

40. **Words**

Spoken words have great power,

They can come back and cause you to cower,

Set a course of action, causing you to fret,

Like a waterfall into a pool of regret,

Restrain your tongue; for angels have also heard,

In anger and slander; stop that spoken word,

Like waters, emotions run deep,

Allow time for Holy Spirit to saturate and seep,

There is only one body, there is no other,

Stop that word; causing harm to a sister or brother,

God's children have many lessons to learn,

Giving voice to anger, Jesus alone you'll spurn,

Actions speak louder than words, I am told,

A word fitly spoken, is like an apple of gold,

And sweet sleep will be your bed,

Allow God to give you peace instead,

Humbly bow a knee, there is no "why"!

For unity in His body, is GOD's heart cry,

41. **Trauma**

When life has spun out of your control,

When the world system has taken a tole,,

When trauma hits the heart of life,

Angels cry with you in your strife,

They lift your prayers to GOD's ears,

Sending spiritual help to ease your fears,

Mercies flow free from GOD's holy throne,

Angels are there helping, your never alone,

Receive Jesus atonement for your own sin,

He'll fight your battle, so you can win,

Fight off those demon attacks with a shrug,

In GOD's arms, receive that Heavenly hug,

42. **Intimate Prayer**

Come Holy Spirit and make me Christ's bride,

Reveal Yourself to me, I have nothing to hide,

Read my heart, it is an open book, so just look,

Renew my youth and give me Your strength,

To make wise choices that give my life length,

Your Shalom peace and the Lover of my soul,

To reside inside to purge and make me whole,

What ever I have left of this life I now live,

Resilience in Christ Jesus, my life I can give,

For the truth of the matter is simply this,

To live my life for Christ, and His Holy kiss,

Free to live without rejections frustration,

No place for shame, guilt or condemnation,

43. **Worship**

GOD goes to and for, seeking hearts,

Coming back to Him, where they start,

A worshiping heart lifts you to Glory,

Releasing GOD's ultimate love story,

Demons will flee with all that is wrong,

Joy is a weapon that keeps you strong,

The LORD loves that one gone amiss,

Returning to worship, is giving GOD a kiss,

Let us lift our hearts to worship the King,

Until we harmonize where angels sing,

For GOD's children love to reminisce,

Then the Holy Spirit returns His kiss,

44. **The Lion**

Do you want to be politically correct,

Or right, with a God who's perfect,

For blessed are the pure in heart,

Your Creator formed you from the start,

Puzzled! Was He really the way to eternal life?

The Son of God, crucified in such strife,

His Disciples became Lions from cowards,

Questioning, but keep going forward,

Tell me, have you already been pruned,

Put to death and Holy Spirit tuned,

Then up from the grave He did arise,

You too can see with Spiritual eyes,

In His body and blood is real wealth,

Communion into supernatural health,

With assurance, the Holy Spirit soars,

For inside you, the righteous Lion roars,

45. Spirit Exercises

Holy whispers invade my being,

Silently waiting for Holy Spirit seeing,

A quiet encounter with my Jesus,

Holding His hand will calm and please us,

To still our thoughts to hear His voice,

It is an early morning choice,

New day beginnings, time to refresh,

Bringing life to bones and health to flesh,

This allows your soul to release,

Fertilize your mind with love, joy, peace,

Tuning in, looking up, hearing clear,

You are precious, loving and forgiving,

Surrendering to Holy Ghost living,

Allow God to give that breath of life,

Breathing deep, releasing strife,

46. **Heaven's Court**

In the courts of Heaven, verdicts are rendered,

Favour in spiritual power to those surrendered,

Trusting in Jesus is a moment to moment choice,

Allowing GOD's powerful life, a voice,

No matter what your circumstances,

Repenting of past and second glances,

Seeking GOD's face is a spiritual action,

Jesus blood, causes Satan's case fraction,

Forgiveness is no ploy, giving tithes with joy,

Not receiving offense is really your defense,

As the Devil roams about making your case,

Through the cross of Christ give him no place,

Heavenly court verdicts are rendered above all,

Intently hear GOD's voice and obeying His call,

Making my spiritual transaction, contender,

For Jesus Christ blood alone is my defender,

47. **What Are You Worth**

God uses rejection to set up your next level,

A higher plan; to stomp on the devil,

As a child come, sit on His knee,

His love will set your heart free,

Only Jesus hugs and Holy Ghost kisses,

Is truly, where real bliss is,

Better to be alone with a child's heart,

Than continually torn apart,

Dare to believe His word,

Listen to God's voice, what you 've heard,

Receive it! Every promise, believe it!

Do what the Lord tells you to do,

Fulfill the plans God has for you,

A child's heart is pure and true,

Catch the vision inside of you,

Release all vengeance, guilt and pride,

Give Christ a clean place to reside,

And you will see what God will do,

He will rise you up and honour you,

48. **A Valentine for Jesus**

Each morning in a Secret Place,

My true Love and I embrace,

Starting my day in a better way,

With a Holy Ghost hug and a Jesus kiss,

Why on earth would I choose to miss,

He opens Heaven to reveal,

My journey and a love so real,

My GOD, my Defender, my Protector,

My Refuge, My Shelter, My Shield,

Safely into Your arms I yield,

My Deliverer, my Health, my Habitation,

My Rest, My Peace, My Salvation,

Always holding Your right hand,

As You lead me into a Freedom land,

GOD's love is so faithful, pure and fine,

For I am His and He is mine,

49. **Life**

Health starts in the spirit man,

Essential union with the Great I AM,

The body apart from the Spirit is dead,

Try living life GOD's way instead,

You take veggies, vitamins and such,

Feed your spirit with the Master's touch

GOD's word is health to all your flesh,

A miracle - body and Holy Spirit mesh,

The Spirit comes in, casting demons out,

Your prayer language you start to spout,

No sin or condemnation will find a place,

Well- being, love, joy, peace will replace,

When Satan's arrows try to take you out,

God fights the battle, so sing and shout,

Now your set apart to do GOD's bidding,

When attacked say, "Are you kidding?"

No matter what the world is selling,

For now you are a Holy Spirit dwelling,

50. **Secure**

Nothing can separate me from GOD's love,

Assurance, when life goes from push to shove,

When tears and torments overwhelm,

And anxiety tries to take the helm,

Repeat GOD's unconditional promise,

GOD's love for you is sure, don't be a Thomas,

Penetrating the soul, pulsing through the heart,

It gives a rejected life a brand new start,

Jesus name is written on every cell,

Strength and boldness GOD's truth to tell,

A whole new being shall emerge,

Convicted, convinced with a Holy Spirit surge,

The love of GOD goes beyond time and space,

For a child of GOD has taken their place,

Comments From the Author

Life consists of broken heart experiences; as long as you give someone else authority over your joy level; you will be on an emotional roller coaster ride until you realize in your own heart that joy is a part of the package you received from Christ when you accepted Him whole heartedly! Come back to your first love and know only GOD can turn your ashes into beauty and He is just waiting on you to give Him permission to do that! Come on a journey that will turn your mourning into dancing!

These poems were Holy Spirit inspired to pass on to heal broken hearts and know intimacy with Jesus Christ will accomplish what no earthly councilor can do, for GOD's word is true and powerful and is going to set you free to be who He has created you to be.

Be blessed and enjoy the ride!

I dedicated this book as a legacy to my children and grandchildren to instill faith in GOD for His promises are true, so trust in GOD not man!

Thank-you to all my Sisters in my prayer group and church family for their encouragement and support!

LOVE IN CHRIST----

Virginia Dickson

NOTES   PRAYERS   DECLARATIONS